Women's Club of Glen Ridge

In Memory of:
Geary Batistini
to the
Glen Ridge Public Library
in 2005.

GARDEN SPIDERS

SPIDERS DISCOVERY LIBRARY

Jason Cooper

www.rourkepublishing.com

PHOTO CREDITS: Title page © James H. Carmichael;
all other photos © Lynn M. Stone

Title page: *Welcome to my web! A Florida garden spider greets its latest victim, a black swallowtail butterfly.*

Editor: Frank Sloan

Cover and interior design by Nicola Stratford

Library of Congress Cataloging-in-Publication Data

Cooper, Jason, 1942-
  Garden spiders / Jason Cooper.
     p. cm. -- (Spiders discovery)
  Includes bibliographical references.
  ISBN 1-59515-447-7 (hardcover)
  1. Black and yellow garden spider--Juvenile literature. I. Title.
  QL458.42.A7C66 2006
  595.4'4--dc22
                                    2005010728

Printed in the USA

CG/CG

Table of Contents

Garden Spiders

The big yellow and gold spiders of gardens and fields are often called garden spiders. These spiders are also known as garden **orb weavers**.

Orb weavers are named for their ability to make large, flat, somewhat round webs of silk. Orb weavers belong to a family of spiders that **arachnologists** call *Araneidae*. All spiders are **arachnids**.

Garden orb weavers are a small group within the orb weaver family. North American **species** include the familiar yellow garden spider, banded garden spider, silver garden spider, and the Florida garden spider.

The largest orb weaver web in the United States is the golden silk orb weaver's.

The best known is the yellow garden spider. It has several nicknames. Among them are golden garden spider, golden orb weaver, banana spider, and writing spider.

A banded garden spider steps closer to its grasshopper prey.

Garden spiders make spectacular webs up to 2 feet (.6 meters) across. Some web strands are sticky. Others are not. A garden spider uses different types of silk for different purposes.

On damp, still mornings, garden spider webs sparkle with dewdrops. Garden spiders don't build lacy webs for beauty, however. The webs are traps for their **prey**.

A yellow garden spider's web sparkles on a dewy morning.

Predator and Prey

Like all spiders, garden spiders are **predators**. They catch and kill other animals. Garden spiders usually eat insects.

Webs usually catch small flying insects. Some of the insects that crash into the web may be twice the size of the garden spider. But that doesn't save their lives.

A banded garden spider waits for an insect to find its web.

A yellow garden spider wraps a small, green insect in silk.

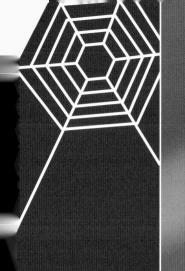

A garden spider drips juices onto prey. The juices soften the flesh of prey, making it liquid. The spider then sucks the liquids and mushy flesh out of its prey.

The garden spider probably cannot see well. It finds its insect victims from vibrations in the web. When an insect becomes tangled, its movements send out vibrations that alert the spider. The spider quickly tiptoes to the victim and wraps it in silk.

Then the spider bites the prey. The bite injects **venom**, which paralyzes and kills. Among the garden spider's victims are aphids, flies, grasshoppers, bees, damselflies, wasps, and mosquitoes.

A garden spider works quickly to wrap a damselfly in silk.

Where Garden Spiders Live

Scientists have identified some 3,000 species of orb weavers. About 160 species live in North America north of Mexico. Yellow garden spiders live from southern Canada south throughout the lower 48 states. They also live in Mexico and south to Guatemala.

Garden spiders do live in gardens, but they live elsewhere, too, in sunny meadows, prairies, and shrubbery.

14

This yellow garden spider lives among autumn wildflowers on a tallgrass prairie.

What Garden Spiders Look Like

Yellow garden spider females are large. They can be slightly more than 1 inch (2.5 centimeters) long. Male yellow garden spiders are much smaller.

Like all spiders, garden spiders have two major body parts. Their head, eight eyes, jaws, and stomach are part of the **cephalothorax**. That's the first section of a spider. The second and larger part is the **abdomen**. Organs such as the heart, lungs, and silk glands are in the abdomen.

A female yellow garden spider is large and handsome.

Both males and females have an egg-shaped abdomen with yellow and black or orange and black markings. Banded garden spiders are striped in black and white.

A bubble of dew gleams on the abdomen of a yellow garden spider at dawn.

19

The Garden Spider's Life Cycle

Female yellow garden spiders lay from 300 to more than 1,000 eggs. They wrap the eggs in a silk **egg sac**.

Perfectly still, a female yellow garden spider waits for a September sun to warm her one last time.

Baby spiders are known as spiderlings. They look much like adult spiders. As the spiders grow during the summer, they make larger and larger webs.

A yellow garden spider guards her egg sac.

Female garden spiders die before or in the first hard frost of autumn. In frost-free places they may live several years. Male garden spiders apparently die soon after mating.

Garden Spiders and People

Despite their large size, garden spiders are a danger only to insects.

Many people who don't like spiders enjoy the beauty of garden spider webs. More people might like the spiders, too, if they knew that garden spiders help keep insect numbers down.

A garden spider web in dew sparkles like jewelry.

Glossary

abdomen (AB duh mun) — the second major part of a spider's body; the section that holds heart, lungs, silk glands, and other organs

arachnids (uh RAK nidz) — spiders and their kin; boneless, eight-legged animals with two major body parts and no wings or antennas

arachnologists (uh RAK nol uh jists) — scientists who study arachnids

cephalothorax (SEF uh luh THOR aks) — the body section of a spider that includes such organs as the eyes, brain, venom glands, and sucking stomach

egg sac (EGG SAK) — a case or container, usually ball-shaped, or eggs

orb weavers (ORB WEEV urz) — any one of several kinds of spiders, most of which spin a flat, somewhat circle-shaped web

predators (PRED uh turz) — animals that hunt other animals for food

prey (PRAY) — an animal that is hunted by another animal for food

species (SPEE sheez) — one kind of animal within a group of closely related animals, such as a *golden* garden spider

venom (VEN um) — a poison produced by certain animals, largely to kill or injure prey

Index

Further Reading

Murawski, Darlyne. *Spiders and Their Webs*. National Geographic, 2004
Squire, Ann O. *Spiders*. Children's Press, 2003

Websites To Visit

http://www.uark.edu/depts/entomolo/museum/argiope.html
http://www.americanarachnology.org/

About The Author

Jason Cooper has written several children's books about a variety of topics for Rourke Publishing, including the recent series *Animals Growing Up* and *Fighting Forces*.